Everything at Once

audrey emmett

illustrations by:
liann sun
flow

ISBN: 978-0692934739

this is for me.
this is for you.
we are one and the same.
we are everything
at once.

contents

DREAMING... 11

REMEMBERING................................... 65

AWAKENING..................................... 111

the collection of words which grew and bloomed on these pages are my unabridged soul. they don't reveal pieces of me, but rather who I am as a whole: my dreams, my memories, and my growing consciousness. though they may tell different tales apart from each other, together they tell one. for in these stories, I found my own. the story of how I realized I could be so much more than what I was allowing myself to be. how I awoke to the truth that I could be everything I ever dreamed I could be. not someday. but now.

for most of my life, I pinned myself down, thinking I had to be one thing or another. but as soon I let go of who I thought I was supposed to be, I awoke to who I knew I could be: my true self. I became everything at once. it felt like freedom in a way that can't be confined to language.

when I was a little girl, the dream of writing was always present, unwavering, in the back of my mind. though forgotten amongst thoughts and doubts that swam on the surface of my consciousness, it was always lingering right below the surface, waiting to break free. I remembered the dream a few years ago, and I reclaimed it. and for a while, that was enough. but when I awakened to the reality of what the dream really could be, and how it set my soul on fire in a way I didn't even know was possible, I knew I had to write this book. for myself. and for you. for others who might feel the same way about their passions. who don't know that they can remember their dream and take it with them into the here and now. and far beyond that. who don't know that when they do this, they can become everything they yearn to be.

our memories, our dreams, and who we are when we are in the present moment are not all separate. they all intertwine to create the person we truly are. the person we see we are meant to be. everything at once.

I share these pieces of language to connect with myself, and I share them to connect with you. when you read this, you will see my soul in its fullness, and we will be connected. not by proximity, but by something much stronger.

my heart skips when I think of you holding this book in your hands, crinkling the pages, folding down corners, getting stains between the words. it excites me, thinking of you underlining phrases and writing in the margins. make this creation your own. because I made this for us.

this book embodies my freedom, my creativity, my spirit, my love. for myself. and for you.

I pray you catch glimpses of yourself when you journey through these pages. I hope you see yourself in the reflection of my tears and in the depth of my consciousness. I dream that you will find an oasis of peace when you reach the end. and I have faith that you will see yourself through my eyes. because if you see any light in me, it is truly a reflection of the light in you.

thank you. for everything. my love for you cannot be defined nor measured. only felt.

you and I, we are here. exactly where we need to be. we are dreaming.

let's make up.

this is for the little girl inside of me who knew she wanted to be a writer from day one. who knew it was her passion and her purpose to create. but was told it was unrealistic.

well, this is my reality.

I created it.

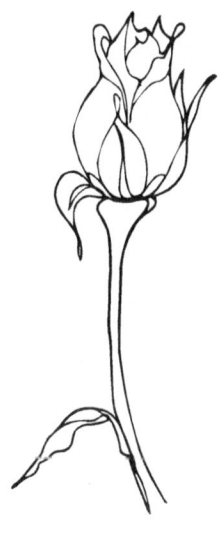

DREAMING

I'll dance with you at sunset. give me golden light and long shadows and I'll fall more in love with you with every step. the long grass brushes my calves like whispers and I can hear the stream running in the back of my mind, but all I see is you. this glow is transforming strands of your hair into gold thread right in front of my eyes and my fingers ache to run through.
there is something magical here.
in the small space between our hands. in the laughter between kisses. in the way your eyes go dark when you see me. in the way the sky's hues are constantly changing. pink and purple and orange and blue. and I give silent thanks for the masterpiece above our heads and the masterpiece in front of me. I don't know if you'll still be here in the glow of the moonlight, but there is something so slow about these moments.

-dreamlike

what scares you?

I am terrified that we are only a moment in this vast universe.
that we are only an atom in this galaxy. less than that. I wish I
could scream and cry and do something that would make a
difference. make a ripple in the world. I'm scared that this
planet is spinning beneath my feet and I'm not doing anything.
that gravity is pinning me down and I want to be free. I want to
paint my hands with stardust so that I will feel like I belong.
where is the edge of the universe? what is beyond that? is that
the place that we go between thoughts? that's what shakes me
to the bone.

fiction is just a beautiful way of telling lies

(fiction flows from every crack in him and spills from every word he breathes)

-*yet I still want to read him from start to finish*

arms struck by lightning
charred her
in teary disgrace

-hurt people hurt

I could never quite apprehend
(or appreciate) what quiet was
but when she appeared with flames
ablaze in her mouth, I understood
that quiet did not always mean peaceful

-if quiet is violent, then she is abusive

little moments inside your mind
I fall in love with you a thousand times
smoke rises like heat
up to the sky
my dreams of you have never died
and only you
could think of love being anything
but romantic
and honestly how could it be
when I am dipping my toes in the pacific
and you are walking home
on the coast of the atlantic

sometimes it hurts to say your name. I can feel it in my chest when I push the syllables forward with my tongue. I can feel the hairline fractures that blanket my diseased heart. it will crumble to dust soon enough. if you only knew the havoc you wreak on me. you were always the only one who could rock me to sleep but now I am up against walls or in my own arms, my hair covering my eyes like a poorly constructed sleep mask. you were always the one for me, but now that it's the other way around, I am not so sure.

-I'm breaking my own heart

I'm chained to hell and locked out of heaven
but I locked my own door because
the gusts of wind were keeping me up at night
so forgive me for not
admiring the swirling black holes
you give my skin
and excuse the fact that
I have tried to swat away
the swishing haze you bathe me in
and please try to overlook that I gaze
at crumbs on counters and cracks on buildings
but I know how it feels to
feel utterly insignificant

-forgive me for the things I've done

fire creeped up my throat when I tried to utter the sweet syllables I knew you were dying to taste. but, my darling, I am a dragon and no matter how hard I try, I cannot let you escape my embrace. because you are my sunrise and my sunset and all the daylight in between. your heartbeat is pressed up against mine, but you've locked yours up and swallowed the key. just like I did to you. just like you did to me. but we put our love to rest long ago, sunk it six feet under. and now, when you bang your fists on my chest, all I hear is thunder. all I feel is hollow electricity. but baby, if you want lightning, if you want fire, my cheeks are full of flames and my lips are dripping with toxicity.

lonely

the   trees in your eyes

lovely

my

sway to the rhythm of   breath

your

they've

I'm starting to think that   had too much to drink

I've

your stormy blue eyes are shattered by tears and I long to seek
refuge in the shadows of your eyelashes

-storm chaser

"if we are a house, my darling, we're being torn down bit by bit.
the rain from our eyes has softened the roof and we've caved,
baby, we've caved. our windows are shattered and blown in by
natural disasters. they were very natural - bound to happen.
we're tearing down the walls in our sleep, not even realizing it.
the floor is going to disappear beneath us, honey, we've got to
escape."

*-I never realized my father was a poet before he said this to my
mother. when I asked what it meant, he just said I'd
understand when I got older. I think I do.*

you are a painting not a person (your colors have just begun to run)

you are a person not a painting (then you are fading away) the oil lanterns illuminate your eyes and his long fingers graze your cheeks and it would be absolutely nostalgic in a black-and-white movie sort of way if his fingers didn't bleed with regrets of past lovers every time he touched you. and coffee drips from his lips in the morning and alcohol from them at night and he sure is well hydrated, you just wish his veins were pumping love instead of toxins as cliché as that sounds because his lips are midnight and you are busy crushing stars as anger drowns out the city blanketing you. and he takes pictures of you but never paints you and it pains you because what if you're not beautiful enough to be put on canvas? you're always aching for something more.

-paris in the moonlight

my relationship with the night changes by the hour.
11 pm and I are just friends
but they can tell that I'm growing fonder of them.
1 am and I are in a budding romance,
opening up like a flower blossoming in the sun,
the moonlight our nourishment.
we are in the honeymoon, moony-eyed phase
and I think I may be in love
with the way the stars wink
and the way the moonlight and streetlight
mix together and pour into the night
like cream into black coffee.
3 am and I are lovers, and I can't get close enough
to the sheets on my bed and I'm clinging
to this shade of sky through sleep deprived eyes.

-I've thrown my anchor into the night but somehow I'm floating towards morning

I truly believe he never *meant* to hurt me. the night was a blur, yes, and I hardly remember the sloppy slurred sentences. I can hardly remember the amber glass shattering above my head and showering down like glitter. I can barely recall the silhouette standing in the doorframe and later, the shadows of trees and headlights passing. I can scarcely picture the curls of smoke passing my shaking breath. and the moon illuminating every heartbeat that jumped from our shirts to meet the other. but my love fills the spaces between his teeth and that night I do remember wondering if I had it backwards: to be afraid of the light instead of the dark. truthfully, I can hardly recollect crossing the highway and feeling lost as the street lamps got fewer and farther between. and I can't be certain, but the sunset might have been quite striking that night.

-do you recall, has he ever hurt you?

the sky comes alive when I speak of you. it paints itself with hues I didn't even know existed outside of my own imagination. I think it loves you more than I do. I look up at how it has set itself ablaze for you, and I wonder if I could ever find it in myself to love you that much. because you deserve so much more than me. all I have to give you is the tainted contents of my heart. but if I could, I would reach up and pluck the sky from its place in the heavens. I would fold it up neatly and give it to you. and you could spread it across your walls, you could hang it from your ceiling. and you could look all around you, you could look at the sky in all its fiery splendor, and you would see how I wish I could love you.

the pool lights made the water glow, and my legs treading underwater were blurred by ripples as I swam closer. his skin seemed gold, almost. a shiny, smooth, pinkish gold that seemed so valuable in the moonlight.

"I'm glad we decided to stay," he whispered, dunking his head under the water and emerging slightly closer to me.

"why are you whispering?" I whispered back, grinning.

"I don't know," he smiled, "it feels weird being here after everyone's left."

"it feels weird being here at night at all," I added, looking around, "but a good weird."

he cocked his head and looked at me, "I agree. . ." he said, his voice trailing off.

my hair was slicked back flat against my head and ran down my back into the pool where it floated behind me, but his blonde locks hung in his eyes. he was close now. close enough that when I reached out, I pushed his hair out his chocolate eyes and back against his head.

both of us treading water were making ripples, which pushed their way to the edge of the pool, without any interruptions.

I was so glad that everyone had gone. there was silence. there was peace. and even though anyone could walk through that gate at any second, I was enjoying watching our connected shadows at the bottom of the pool in the quiet.

there was always an unspoken something between us. and I don't think either of us knew what it was, or what its boundaries were. so, when I pulled him closer and let my chlorine-tasting lips melt into his, I knew it was half-wrong and half-right. I just didn't know it would feel so damn intoxicating.

-an excerpt

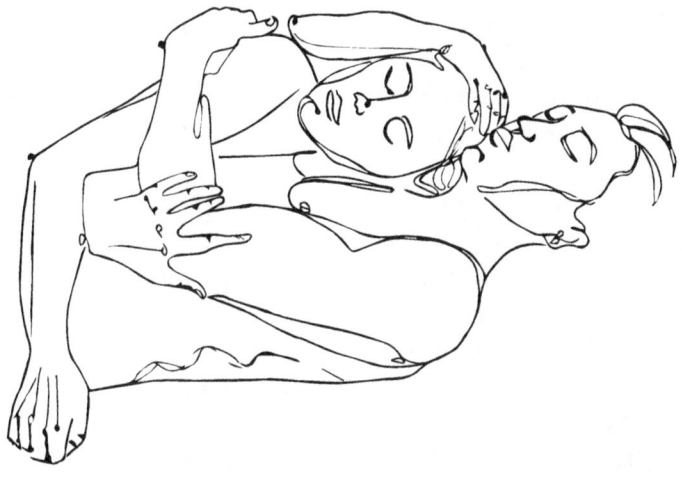

I slide my fingers past your ribs and my head fits perfectly
between your chest and your head and we make a home there.
in the spaces between.

-untruth

"stop! . . . just stop," she hesitated. and he found the most pathetic scrap of hope in that hesitation. he could fit so many "I love you's" in that bit of space in her speech. but he didn't. he just sat there dumbly and watched her steer them into a wall; watched them crash and burn.

he put his face in his hands and rubbed like he wanted to rub off his identity. everything he was that she didn't love anymore.

he felt a cold hand on his, trying to pry his fingers off his face. "hey . . . hey," she put her other hand on the back of his neck and leaned forward so her forehead touched his. he felt warmth and dreams and gold when they touched, but he knew she only felt skin on skin.

he opened his eyes. she wasn't even crying. how could she not be crying?

she leaned away slowly and slid her hands off his neck. his skin tingled.

"why . . .?" he rasped. he didn't even want to know. he just knew he had to keep talking. had to keep moving his lips. because once this conversation was over, so were they.

she sucked in a bit of breath. looking at him with a mixture of bewilderment and pain, she just shook her head slowly. she started to stand up and he reached for her hands frantically, "please don't go. please."

she yanked her fingers out of his grasp. "I can't do this," she whispered, staring at him. her eyes were hauntingly hollow. he didn't even recognize her. and he doubted she recognized him in this state. they were just two strangers. except one was in love.

she turned to leave. "I don't know you," he croaked out. and she pretended not to hear.

-an excerpt

if I tipped my heart forward, do you know what would spill out? would you catch the tangled contents in the palms of your hands? or would you leave spaces in between your fingers so the darkness would leak out and you were only left with my fiery and flashing love for you? would you even hold out your hands at all? or would you feel the warmth in your hands, see it glowing lightly, with all the possibilities of what we could be, and let it run through your fingers and drip all over my toes? or even worse, would you place both hands over my chest and beg me to hold my heart still, to drain it of all the adoration, and tuck it away, somewhere where you'll never be able to find it?

"*I still love her*" is written all over his stomach and he is not ashamed. he is proud of his work, his ability to admit what others aren't. "*I should have kissed her longer*" is painted up and down his legs, but he does it quickly. like pen to skin is a burning match. "*I couldn't save her*" is scrawled on one arm and "*without her the world is a blur*" is scribbled on the other. "*this is not my home*" is written in small neat block letters between his shoulder blades. "*she is my home*" is scratched shakily everywhere else, blanketing his back. his need to speak is now nonexistent. everything he wants to say is merely a shadow compared to the sun that is her.

-body language

your voice blends perfectly
with the piano.
and your callused fingertips
trace my knee, out of focus and achingly familiar.
these four walls
are home to so much pain.
the flames licking the wall
wipes it all away.

his teeth chattered and his breath sputtered
and his hands shook and somehow finding this
endearing made her a monster
when he gasped
she swiped his breath and left him
with a fragile smile on his lips
so he shielded the knowledge
that this beautifully insane creature
whose mind held ideas that mortals could never fathom
also grasped his strings
he was her puppet waiting
for a command from the voice that was slowly
slitting his throat

-*"we're detrimental but you needn't worry"*

I want to set someone's world on fire. I want to make them feel everything at once, their heart hot. they can't control themselves around me. they run their hands through their hair and sigh. and I smirk shamelessly, knowing they can't resist, knowing I have them. I have their heart strings in between my fingers and I am playing with them. fiddling with them just enough so they won't think I'll pull.
but that's when I do.

the sun is an eye
the moon is another
dark always plays light

you're not dead,
time just took back the years it burdened you with

you're not alive,
time is just being generous

-time is a knife with a softer name

he

has charcoal dust on the tips of his ears and perpetual ink stains
on his fingers. and it seems the only tangible correlation
between him and her is their love of beauty, but they are
looking from different angles. alas, he still gazes at her soft
features, her green eyes, how they beg to settle down on paper.
he is convinced he would never do her justice.

she

prefers colored pencils because she knows she is good at
making mistakes. she also knows the dark eyes that seem to
search her, looking for something she knows they won't find.
she likes tangible things. things she can hold onto with both
hands. she knows love is more abstract than that.

they
both paint a very different picture.

in dreams he is mine, and when I wake up he is everywhere. in my dreams we meet, though underneath all the hello's, how are you's, all the small talk, there is recognition. there is familiarity. and somehow everyone is caught up in a merry-go-round of colorlessness. of routine. but we are different. he understands my thoughts, though he barely understands his own. we fall into step with each other very quickly. and while everyone is still going round and round, he knows what to order me for dinner, and that I can't stand camping, and exactly what to do to cheer me up. we are advancing while everyone else is stuck in the same old place. in my dreams, he is everything. but then I wake up. and he is gone.

the cold
nips at your nose
and your warm breath
billows out of your mouth
and collides with the cold morning air
like smoke.
your face is pale.
and your nose bright red.
the snowflakes are landing
lightly
on your curls.
there is a drop of coffee
on the side of your lips.
you look as though
there should be a halo
suspended above your head
(but I know better than that),
yet I think I've fallen in love already.
just looking at you.

he always smelt of daffodils and buttercups like the faded ones on his little sister's bedspread. and when his words became sharp, his green eyes grew dim because his father was the only role model he ever had and he knew that when his voice sliced into my skin, he was just a mirror of the man who raised him. my hands were dripping with blood when I tried to fix him; they slipped every time I grazed his broken heart. and my chest tightened more and more with every mistake, with every grating whisper aimed directly at me. they hit the bullseye every damn time.

-I regret everything and nothing in the same breath

there's always a stack of books on her nightstand, along with a few diaries, though she hates when you call them that. she prefers the word journal. thinks it makes her sound sophisticated, like she wears glasses and sensible shoes. she sleeps soundly in the night and lightly in the morning, her chocolate hair a tangle and her lips slightly parted. where you see sunsets, she sees opportunities. and climbs on roofs, her long legs stretched out in front of her. looking completely at peace, she takes polaroid photos and scribbles poetry in the fleeting light. she is a highway, from moving extremely fast and incredibly loud, to a standstill in a second. sometimes she will be cold. she will freeze you out like you can't believe and your fingers will feel ready to fall right off. but the next moment she will take them in hers and give you an easy smile and all will seem right with the world once again. she likes to think of herself a daredevil, and she is, oh believe me, she is. but she hates to admit she is afraid of a few crawly legs and a pair of small wings. if you kill it quickly, you will see thankfulness painted all over those ruddy cheeks. she adores to wake up before the sun, so don't be alarmed if you hear the coffee machine running at 5am. she likes physical affection, even if she doesn't like to admit it. touch her when no one else can see. if you take her to the beach, you'll see her beauty. with the wind getting lost in her hair and the sun gracing and kissing her pale skin. but if you take her to the city, you'll see her happy. at home nestled in a small room among millions of other people. I think that it makes her feel small, but in a good way. in a way that makes her feel not so important and not so responsible. she'll always take your hand and lead you, even if she doesn't know the way. being able to love someone like that is a miracle. she's a miracle, down to the curve of her neck and the freezing of her fingers. if you wish to see her sleeping soundly in the night, and see her hazel eyes open every morning, I suggest you remember how lucky you are. but with a girl like that, it's hard to forget.

I closed the door quietly, which I never do. and for some odd reason, I didn't call to her like I always do when I get home. I sauntered into the kitchen, but with an apprehensive feeling hanging over my head, waiting to drop. and that's when I saw it. in the rough light of 6:02, she was gazing, intensely and intently, at her reflection. I watched her turn back and forth, walk closer and farther away from herself, pinching and pulling. she was exposed, almost completely. she grazed her porcelain skin with her tiny fingertips and winced, like it hurt her to feel what was living just beneath the surface. soon, tears began to roll down her cheeks like my car down the driveway every morning. pair after pair, she tried on jeans, the waistband warming the beautiful dimples on the small of her back. she dropped down to her knees and her gorgeous features completely crumpled and my heart mirrored that. her hands were placed in front of her, furling and unfurling, pressing the ground so that she might fall through. I soon realized I was on my knees too.

-objects in mirror are closer (to breaking) than they appear

poetry makes it seem that everything tragic happens at night, in the dim glow of the alarm clock, but I find that alarmingly false. the most devastating things in life happen in the late afternoon light when dust particles float in the air. the most terrible events occur in the harsh glare of sunlight. you left me during the day, the sun blaring and bright. my heartbeat was jumping through my shirt, reaching out to meet yours and I remember wondering how my heart could still pound, how I could feel what I feel, knowing your heart wasn't reaching out anymore. your footsteps still echo in my ears as you walked down my stairs, but my bare feet were heavy on the carpet, still warm from the setting sun.

we are slow dancing in a snowfall, the crystalline flakes getting caught between us. all I can see amongst the swirl of ice is the glow of embers lost in your eyes. they tell me something that your mouth cannot. so we vanish to a room warmed by candles, whose flames dance to the rhythm of our breath. and I am loving you head to toe. down to the fever of your soul. we create sparks between our lips, whispers of something greater, something more powerful. you kiss my body with such electricity that my nerves catch fire. and I pour kisses upon your skin with all the fervor in my bones. and as the snow spills from the heavens, blanketing this room, we erupt into nothing but flames.

-*heatwave*

I asked her to marry me on a thursday. over the hum of the heater and over the pitter patter of the rainfall. I asked her as she was leaving for work. her hair was folded in on itself and her blouse was tucked into that skirt that fit perfectly around her hips. I asked her in the kitchen. in my sweatshirt with the holes in it that she likes to put her fingers through and with the oil stain on the shoulder. I asked her with my hair all tousled and cereal on the corners of my mouth and sleep still in my eyes. not because I was planning on it. but because she always said that you find the most extraordinary things in the most ordinary places.

I've said, "I love you"
to many faces
and many places
I've left little crumbs
of my heart
on street corners
and in people's hands
eyes that match
the misty rain
don't leave me
dangling
I've learned to love fiercely
and leave
but still
I hope they make imprints
on your palms

I dreamt about you last night. just as I dream about you every night. all I remember was smoke floating past my lips and expecting my head to get all fuzzy. but as my fingers started to ache from the cold, I realized I didn't feel anything. and while others around me started to dance with their heads tilted back to the sky, howling like wolves, I just sat there, staring at them. my head was immersed in a cloud of hazy smoke and my nose ran from the cold. then, all of the sudden, snow was up to my ankles and there you were, reciting language in a beautiful tongue to a girl who would never appreciate the words that spilled from your mouth the way I did. freezing, and enamored with you. you stole away from her somehow (I don't quite remember) and together you and I rode a chair lift up and up, towards the dusty pink and orange sky. and my cheeks were ruddy from the cold. but they matched yours perfectly.

"why do we fall in love, knowing heartbreak is inevitable? it's like jumping out of an airplane, knowing you don't have a parachute. but, hey, if you get lucky, you might land on your feet." her gaze shifted to his eyes and she pulled her knees to her chest, guarding herself slightly.

"well, what does landing on your feet look like?" he inquired, tilting his head and trying to dig a little before she clammed up again.

"well, marriage, in theory," she replied. she looked down at her knees again and felt the salty air blow across her cheeks. looking up to see the curtains fluttering in the breeze, she got up to close the window, thinking that maybe it would be easier to shut herself off too.

he let his eyes rest on her face and debated whether or not to crack a joke. because in the end, they were just two emotionally closed off people who would probably end up in therapy later in life anyway. but just as the punch line began to pass his lips, he switched gears, "I think landing on your feet looks like finding a soulmate, regardless of the outcome."

her body startled with surprise. then, after a minute of silence, of contemplation, she nodded once. "okay," she muttered quietly, a soft smile materializing on her lips.

a gentle smile appeared on his face simultaneously, as he wondered how he got so lucky to see this bit of sky in an otherwise storm of a girl.

- *an excerpt*

her dark hair she dyed yellow, the color of that blonde girl that every boy she'd ever known was desperately in love with. she painted her plain nails light pink, the color of pepto bismol. the boys she'd grown up with suddenly began to talk to her. offer her drinks at parties. offer her rides in their pickup trucks. she sometimes accepted, sometimes declined. she was a mystery to every single one of them. they wanted more. she wanted so much less. "she's got a pretty face," she heard one of them remark. "I bet she's got a multitude of sins lyin' beneath those baby blues," another one added. she heard the smirk in his voice. her hands shook as she fought the urge to take the wheel and just go. just drive. just let her wheels eat road until she hit water. then take a sharp right and chase ocean. and chase waterfalls. but honks and the smell of burnt rubber bring her back to her bottle-blonde life in Brad-from-chemistry's car. and she aches to cut all her ties, let her roots grow out, scratch the dreadful pink from her fingernails.
and let go.

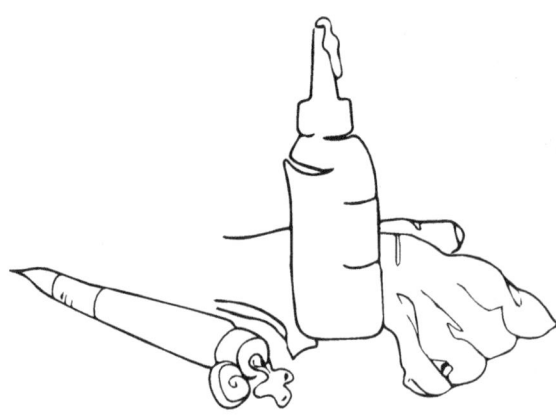

she had a birthmark like a globe on her hip
and he had always liked to travel

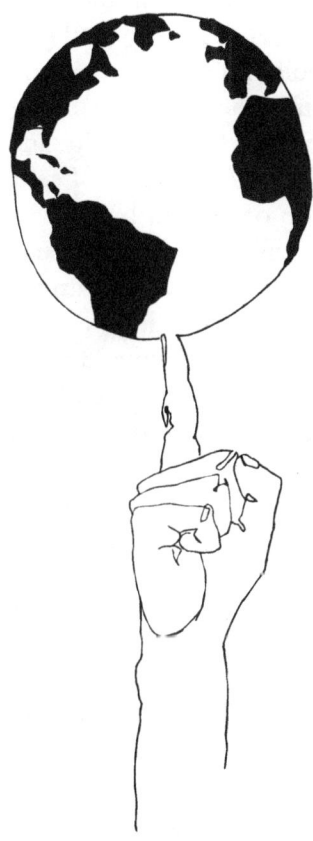

all I want is to be in a coffee shop, writing, and have a fantastic freckled boy approach me and ask my name. we will talk like we've known each other for years, like we've known each other our whole lives. over empty coffee cups and dishes littered with crumbs, we will marvel over the wonderment of it all. over the beauty of two strangers who've found each other, who steady each other. and even later, when a waitress will tell us they're closing and we will see the day has passed us by without our noticing, we won't want to say goodbye just yet. so we will roam new york city in the rain and in the dark. everything will be blurry around the edges, just fuzzy and perfect and I can't wait any longer. so I pull him under an overhang and lean in close to catch his lips in mine. he will walk me home, and holding hands with him will feel just right. and weeks later, on a checkered picnic blanket in the middle of central park, my heartbeat will fall on top of his and I will write poems up and down his arms and we will fall in love in the complete stillness of the moment, with the city moving all around us. and even in the harsh light of a drugstore at 2 am, he will think I look more beautiful than ever, without makeup and my tangled curls atop my head, threatening to spill right off. and in the apartment we share, we will stick sticky notes on the windows and light switches informing each other of our fondness for one another, along with inside jokes scrawled messily on the back. and he will play with my hands when we are watching movies, pressing his lips against my palms and leaving trails of kisses up and down each finger. he will understand me and make me laugh until my stomach hurts. he will tell me I'm gorgeous when he catches me staring at the mirror for a bit too long. and after late nights, we'll wake up in our bed leaning against the city, our fingers still sloppily intertwined and our hearts beating in time. we can cook and journal and read and explore and miss the stars together. and he'll love me enough to scream with me in the moonlight but he won't hold a grudge in the morning. the highline is our place. the whole city is our place. it knows us and our love. heat will be expensive in the winter so we'll pile up blankets around us and tangle our bodies together. and he'll stick love notes (with my name enclosed in a heart at the top) in the pockets of my clothes when he's folding laundry. sometimes there will be flowers on the toilet seat (just to surprise me), always daisies because he'll know they're my favorite. and other times he'll just look at me. in the back of taxis and across crowded rooms or empty ones, with music playing or in complete silence. and just say my name. and we'll tumble and fall in love all over again. he'll kiss my wrists and behind my ears and in the dark hours of the morning when delirium is the only thing keeping us awake, I'll try to count all the freckles on his face and fail miserably. silences will be comfortable with him, no stilted awkwardness. only our breaths filling the spaces between us. and the air will be chock full of maybe's and what if's and adventure will be staring us right in the face. we'll lay on our cool kitchen floor on scorching summer days, our bodies stretching across inches that feel like miles and fight aimlessly, pausing every now and then to dissolve into laughter. and he'll be smart and he'll challenge me but not to the point where we don't understand each other. we will sit on rooftops and watch sunrises together, the sun kissing us but there is no comparison to the way he'll kiss me when the sun is halfway between the sky and the skyscrapers.

-my imagination runs wild and takes me with it

I was laying on my back on the sun soaked sheets and my fingers were dancing in the air to the record player's sweet song. it was the same music all summer long. always harps. he took a drag of a cigarette and soon my fingers were accompanied by swirling smoke that curled right above my eyes. I glanced at his profile lying next to mine and I wondered when the next time he would ask me if I wanted a smoke was. I wondered when the next time I would have to decline would be. sun filtered through the blinds delicately and I held my hand up to the light, watching the glowing strings make designs and shadows over the small hazy room. he lazily blew smoke into the air again and I turned over, facing away from him. the summer was almost over and I knew that in the fall, he'd still be here, doing the same exact thing. except that the sunlight would be more golden somehow and it would sink below the trees much earlier in the evening. and I knew that I would be off somewhere doing something much different than this and that thought had always comforted me. except that now it didn't. the smoke was still dancing above me, but my fingers weren't there anymore. and so I lifted them up, and as soon as they touched the golden light, I reached over and took the cigarette from his mouth. I put it to my lips.

I have heat locked in my lips

-you set me on fire

she hopped up on the counter, butt first. "what about brownies?" she inquired, "we could make brownies." she shifted things around in the cabinet, pots and pans clanging loudly in the night.

he glanced at the glowing numbers above the stove: 3:04. "I don't know . . . I mean - it's late and -"

"it is not!" her eyes darted to a different clock, a fancy meteorologist one hanging above the window. the moonlight outside filtered through the trees, past the window pane, and lit up her face. "that clock says sunrise is at 7:27 . . . AM!" she added for good measure. a goofy smile spread across her mouth and soon he found his face mirroring hers.

"screw it. let's make brownies."

she let out a small cheer and began tying a "kiss the chef" apron around her neck and waist.

making brownies soon proved to be not as exciting as she made it out to be, and he could tell she was losing interest quickly. her eyelids drooped and so did her body, against the countertop and against him. "do you want me to make coffee?" he asked, "it could go well with the brownies. or fudge, rather," he said, glancing down at the batter.

she shook her head sleepily and walked away, down the hall, into the darkness of the house. her little footsteps echoed in the hallways. she returned with heaps of blankets upon blankets and spread them out all over the kitchen tiles. without a word, she flopped down on the kitchen floor and promptly fell asleep.

she was lying on her stomach, so her body rose and fell every time a small snore escaped her lips. he leaned down, untying the apron from around her neck so she wouldn't choke.

he hesitated. then, against all judgment, he decided to obey the apron's instructions. he kissed her, softly, behind her ear. "what am I going to do with you?" he whispered, smiling faintly.

-an excerpt

it was still dark out when he felt a small palm in the middle of his shoulder blades. it walked its fingers up to his neck and tickled until he got goosebumps and shivered.

he opened one eye. all he saw were clocks lining the walls and dark pine trees crowding the windows. then a pair of chocolate rimmed lips appeared above him. then a nose. then dark lashes encircling bright green eyes.

"it's still dark out," he whispered sharply.

"so?"

"so, dark is the time for sleeping. not eating the brownie batter you were too tired to finish a couple hours ago."

"but, why sleep when you can be awake?" she leaned in close to him so he could smell the chocolate in her breath. he felt an uneasy turning in his stomach. the soft spot behind her ear still lingered on his lips.

"besides," she said mischievously with a glint in her eye and a half smile playing on her mouth, "I wanted to talk to you." she laid down next to him, her face facing his.

"last night," she continued. "I heard something in my ear . . . something like a small sigh."

his face heated up considerably, "I was untying the apron so you wouldn't choke."

"but, you see, I recognized the sigh. it was a sort of happy sigh. the sigh that you sigh - or anybody sighs, for that matter - after a kiss."

"it was just - just behind the ear. just . . . just good-night." he avoided her gaze, furrowing his brows.

a strange look appeared on her face. she inched closer to him. then, acting on the impulse of her sleep deprived heart, she whispered, "then this is good morning." and kissed him gently. and as the sun started to creep over the horizon, she laughed into his lips and pulled away, smiling.

7:27, he thought, glancing at the clock, *right on schedule.*

-an excerpt (the continuance)

there were words written back and forth on his guitar but they were worn down slowly by his fingers and their endless playing he struck the strings with all the gentleness of a whip and I love it his guitar I mean how it was always with him and how he would pick at the strings absentmindedly in coffee shops when we would talk about his music and suddenly he would get an idea for a song and start scratching it down on my arm or a napkin and I would think this is what teetering on the edge of a cliff feels like because if I moved or even looked at him in those green eyes that reminded me too much of dark forests my heart would be the beat of his next rock song and I would be falling or I would wake up

bleak clouds coalesce
glitter pours from the heavens
morning light draws close

-the first time

there you are
your fingers spread wide
blades of grass and a couple daises
poking through
in the spaces between
and a sliver of bare skin exists
between my top and shorts
I can feel the grass tickling my back
lightly
they say
time flies when you're having fun
but I wonder if
it's the opposite
because in this moment
time is frozen
and I stretch this moment with sticky fingers
so it lasts forever
and I am here, I am here, I am *here*
and I could not be happier

"what do you imagine our future looking like? . . . feeling like?" he asked me one morning, tracing the skin on my back with fingers wet from the ocean. every time I would doze off, a droplet would drip from his hair onto my back, sliding down my skin and onto the sheets, waking me up all over again.

I was all awake now. and his question aroused curiosity in me. he had never inquired about the future before. we both seemed to make a habit of nesting in the moment.

I turned over, onto my back, and his hands never left my body, curling around my waist and then onto my stomach. I gazed up at him lovingly, his hair matted and soaked and salty. and his tan skin luminous, grains of sand clinging to it. his eyes, though bright, were still sleepy and I knew mine matched his perfectly.

"this," I told him honestly, my heart swelling with every beat. I reached up and carefully brushed the sand off his eyebrows and eyelashes, hearing it rain down on the duvet.

"c'mon . . ." he said, smiling and nuzzling into my neck.

"I'm serious!" I laughed and cupped his face in both my hands. I made sure he was looking me in the eyes, "you. and me. that's all I need . . ." I paused, brushing my nose against his and humming tenderly, "it's so much more than enough."

he sighed happily and flopped down beside me, on his back. and we looked up at the ceiling, where, last summer, we had painted a mural of the sun setting over the ocean. for the first few nights after that, paint had dripped on us while we were sleeping, and I had awoken with droplets of sunshine on my bare back.

he interlaced my fingers with his and we both looked at our hands tangled together. "this?" he whispered softly. and I felt, in that moment, that I held his heart in my hands. I could feel it beating.

"this."

-an excerpt

REMEMBERING

at age 9, her tummy stuck out, similar to her two front teeth, but mirrors just held a reflection, and there was no subtext lying right below the glass. her hair spiraled out from her head, and her voice was slightly unhinged, but in a sweet way that made boys turn their heads. *by age 12*, she had learned that people were not so forgiving of the skin that spilled over her jeans, but she turned her cheek so their whispers trailed off her jaw, not reaching her ears. *by age 13*, she had lost fat but was now weighed down by the fluorescent lights that lined the speckled ceilings of doctor's offices. their eyes swept over her reproachfully and her hair was now tied back and she never let it out. *at age 14*, she burns and pulls her hair so it lies flat against her skull and her voice is still sweet, but boys don't turn their heads anymore.

the words she uttered never
quite aligned with her thoughts
her tongue moved and her mouth
exhaled sentences
but they were empty and hollow
she longed to recite the thoughts
that crowded and jumbled her brain
that pumped through her veins
so she etched the words she ached
to speak onto her skeleton

-(she wasn't living,
simply existing, therefore she was dead)

the pounding rain
on my bedroom window
seems appropriate
considering how
there happens to be
a violent downpour
occupying my body
considering how
the heavy droplets
it so generously gives
are leaking out of my eyes
dribbling down my cheeks
despite my efforts to bare a bright grin
and the tiny sun I carry
on my ankle
seemed such a brilliant idea
before this thunder
and lightning storm
took shelter inside my brain
but there was no storm warning
no sirens
to gear me up
and there's no sunlight
nor rainbow in sight

the day I stumbled across a picture of myself in your wallet was the day I realized I loved you. not dreamy, fairytale infatuation, but clear, real, after-the-credits-roll love. the kind of love you look straight in the eye because you're not scared of it anymore. of what it could be. or maybe you look it dead in the eye because you are scared. but the only way in is in. and when I saw my face staring up at me in between the dollars and cents, that's what I did. I looked at myself in my pupils, in my corneas, in my irises, and I fell in love with you. and everything inside of me swung from black and white to color. but when night started to bleed into day and dawn was all we had left, I wanted to hold onto that moment and never let it go. but time rushed through my fingers like water because what are we holding onto, really? not time. not 11:11's or 4:44's or 10:13's. not something so abstract that it slithers in and out of your brain like snakes. we're holding onto each other's hands. and maybe that's all love is, really. it's not holding onto those dollars and cents. but the picture in between.

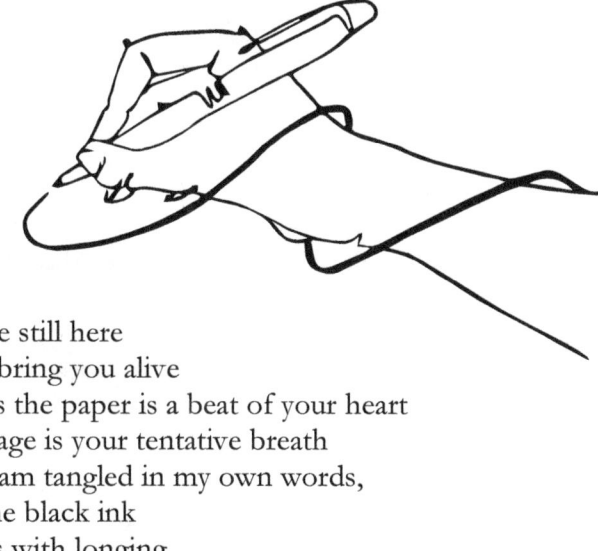

I write about you
and it's as if you are still here
strokes of my pen bring you alive
every time it strikes the paper is a beat of your heart
every flutter of a page is your tentative breath
and after a while I am tangled in my own words,
wrapped around the black ink
and my heart aches with longing

say you will
say you won't
heaven and hell on the same ends of the spectrum

I say I'll take away your pain
but I only say it in vain
thinking you will do the same

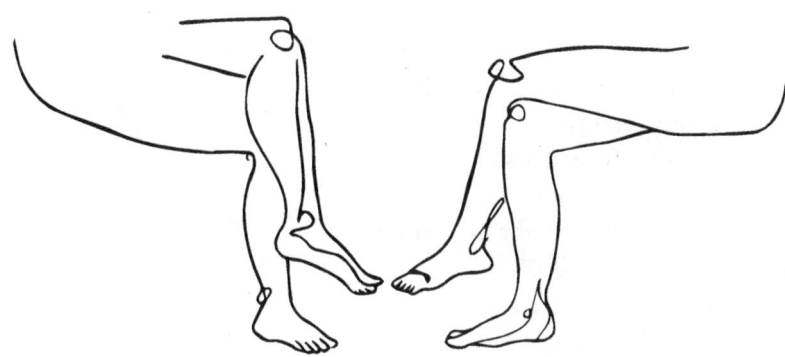

time makes sure I miss you
though I don't know how
you were a room full of
smoke and mirrors
and everywhere I turned
I saw myself:
faded, trapped
you were fool's gold
you looked real
but you burned me
until my skin turned to ash
you branded me
with your fingertips
and your whispers
while the moonlight lit you up
and made you look
safe
one hand held mine
while the other crossed its fingers
behind your back

-trust is translucent and you are awfully opaque

have you ever been in love?

I think that I have preconceived ideas of love in my mind and I think that, in the heat of the moment, I mistook the knots in my chest for something resembling the love. I think I've loved but never been in love, if that makes sense. and I think I've fallen, but never in love. only on the pavement with scrapes and scars on my hands. and I think it's strange that red is the color associated with love and it's also the color of blood.

seconds turn into
minutes
turn into
hours
turn into
days

anticipation

waiting for the words that will
never come

I mistook bullets for fireworks

her name was Mary and she worked in an office building. you
brought her up like it was nothing. like we were nothing. we
were sitting across from each other at the dinner table when
you told me all about her, generous adjectives spilling from
your mouth onto your untouched spaghetti. you told me how
you were so fond of how she got ready in the morning. all
routine and meticulous. I am certain I shrunk in that moment.
so messy and raw as I sat there with my curls piled atop my
head and paint streaked across my face and charcoal
underneath my fingernails. I remember feeling jealousy tear
into the soft skin of my heart, its unforgiving teeth branding me
with her very existence. you sat there, your eyes, dreamy pools
of desire, letting your tongue wrap around her name. letting the
letters get caught in your teeth. my fists held beads of sweat as I
tried to repress the urge to hand you some floss or a damn
toothpick. because when you talked about her . . . *Mary*. the
deep chasm of our differences widened between us. I wanted to
close it. I wanted to sew it shut. I wanted you to let me kiss you
so hard that the perfect memory of her would shatter and fall
to pieces inside your brain. but I was so afraid. that the
moment my mouth met yours I would taste her on your lips.
because I knew my tongue would touch the millions of things
that you and her were. that we never will be. because I know I
take your world off its hinges but she is lost to you. a fictitious
creature woven from vague memories and soft dreams. but I
loved you wilder than she ever did. but maybe that's all there is.
is wild love and lost hope. and over cold spaghetti, my untamed
tenderness for you dried up. and we became lost as well.

it's 11:16 am and it's thursday and when the streetlight
streaming through my window woke me up at 5:57 am
I honestly did not expect a freight train to run over my heart.
but here we are (or here I am) at 11:18 am and three minutes
ago I passed you and your voice and your eyes and your
freckles and you said, "I love you desperately."
I turned around, half-expecting you to be talking to me. but
you weren't and I wish (desperately) that I was on the other line
of that phone call.
but here I am (and here you aren't) and
I just hope that even at 4:09 am when
I miss you so much my head is spinning.
I hope she's staring down at her hands wondering
what she did to deserve you.

how do you feel?

well, that's a loaded question, now isn't it? I feel as if I've stumbled across a secret, his hands grazing mine. I've sucked in too many breaths to feel this steady on my feet. I should feel lightheaded and feel guilt in my mouth as heavy as lead. but I just feel mixed up inside, as though the sentences spilling off my tongue are alphabet soup and some letters are stuck to the roof of my mouth. my lungs are filled with feelings that, if tested, would tip the scale towards magic. chills explode like miniscule bombs back and forth across my skin whenever his eyes collide with mine. I don't feel that when I hold *his* hand and for that I am both sorry and not sorry at all.

he is heaven
poured into a human mold

I breathe words like oxygen
but your words like smoke

I've downed three
and by my fourth
here lies my dignity
and the static in my heart
because your bleary-eyed confusion
told me more about myself
than the lines on my palms
so now I'll reclaim my disheveled heart
and I'll unravel the knots in my stomach
I'll surrender the roses I've held captive in my cheeks
and the dark crescent moons that
orbit just beneath my eyelashes
suddenly
I'm sober for the first time since
I met you(r eyes)

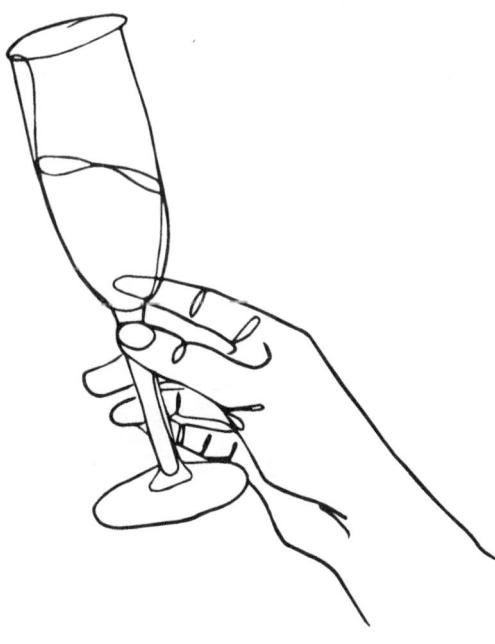

the way he said my name
he made it sound like a prayer

-*yet I was the one to fall to my knees*

I need you as much
as I wish I didn't

you let me drive you home in your old jeep because you'd had much too much to drink and I was the closest person to the door. you have no idea how fast my pulse was racing as I gripped your steering wheel. so tight my knuckles turned white. you fell asleep and my heart dipped as soft snores escaped your lips. and I tried to avoid every bump and hole in the road as to not stir you awake. you have no idea how many goosebumps covered my skin as I tried to keep my eyes on the road and not trained on your face. what a privilege it was to see this in the moonlight. how different this was than under florescent bulbs. how thankful I was that I was sitting so close to you. how beautiful 2 o'clock can be next to be someone you love.

there are intricate details
and fine lines
between caring for someone
and loving them
and I plan to wipe them all away

audrey emmett

her hands were far too small
for red solo cups

I cut my hair a week ago because I couldn't stand to have your fingerprints linger between the strands but you somehow seeped through and now there's a virus raging through my mind and it's not a coincidence that it has the same name as you

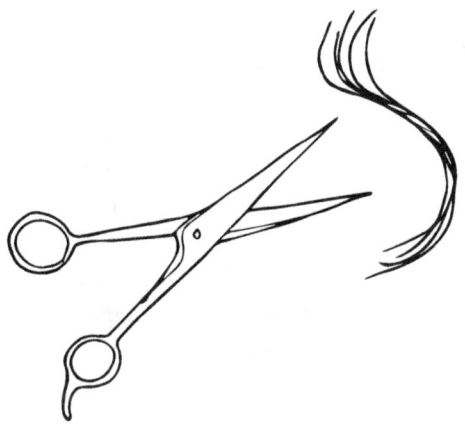

it's two years later. you see a beautiful woman walking down the street. her hair is long and flowing caramel and her legs go on for miles. she is gorgeous but you feel this gaping hole inside of you deepen the same way it's been deepening ever since you left her. you know you dug that hole, and someday you'll have to lie in it. so you let the beautiful girl go. like you've let every other one go, sooner or later. because this hole is swallowing you whole.

it's five years later. you haven't gotten a good night's sleep in months and caffeine is the only thing keeping you awake. your eyes are rimmed with red and dark crescent moons lay right below. you enter the coffee shop in which you are now a regular. and in your favorite window seat, right next to the plush couch, sits a little miracle. her hair is shorter, and she looks younger and older at the same time. her eyes are even greener, if that's possible. maybe they're magnified by her new glasses, that frame her round, beautiful face. she sips tea and is writing, her nose all scrunched up. and you notice, like you'd notice a bomb in the coffee shop, a man seated next to her. both their hands are underneath the table, connected. you inhale sharply and feel darkness shroud you; the only light is her. you feel her name taking shape in your mouth and suddenly it leaps from your lips, but your voice sounds far away and deeply pained. she looks up, eyebrows raised and lips slightly parted. her brow furrows when she recognizes you, but it takes her a second to remember your name, which twists the knife further. but when she says it, it feels like every person who has ever said those two syllables has been saying it wrong. because the way it rolls off her tongue and tumbles past her lips is nothing but right. she stands up and hesitates, but then strides over and hugs you. her touch feels like magic and you hold on tighter than you ever have before. she pulls away first, of course, and offers to introduce you to her - deep breath - fiancé. and you know that this is the space in the dialogue where you are supposed to say of course, but you can't. so you pretend as though she had not mentioned the fact that she would soon be married and you offer to buy her a cup of green tea. she looks pleased you remembered. and before she can say so, you tell her of course you remembered, how could you forget anything about her? she looks uneasy and briefly glances back over at the man at the table. she declines the tea. you smile like your insides aren't hollow. you voice the fact that you would love to catch up and she tucks a strand of hair behind her ear and fiddles with the ring on her finger. it looks an awful lot like the ones you've been eyeing in the windows for the past five years, dreaming. she looks back at the man once more, hesitates a second longer, then agrees. you can feel the smile growing larger on your face and she laughs a little, one that sounds like music. and you want to kiss her and hold her so badly it physically pains you. but instead you just suggest this coffee shop at this time tomorrow. and she nods, another victory. she touches your shoulder lightly and you feel hope filtering into your body, slowly but surely. she looks down at the floor when she says that she hopes you know that she is engaged. to be married. and that seeing you tomorrow does not change any of that. you smile and nod like that is obvious. and she looks relieved. what a wonderful thing. for her to be relieved that you will not kiss her. the hope slowly drains.

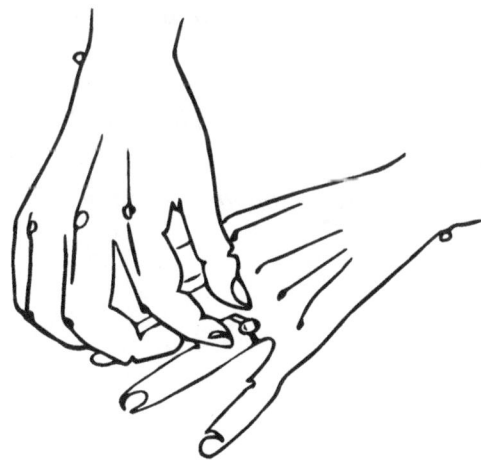

here's your coffee mug. I don't want it. I don't want to think about how you came downstairs in the mornings after you'd stayed over and used the same one every time. how you made and poured the coffee, how you went into the fridge and the cabinets to get milk and sugar. all like you lived there. you were just a bit too comfortable. a bit too routine. like you thought you'd be doing this forever. your lips touched this mug more times than I can count. I don't want to think about kissing you anymore than I already do.

here are your sunglasses. they bring me right back to your convertible. your hand on my thigh and our voices intertwined, singing along to the radio. my laughter ringing out louder than when you revved the engine. I don't want to remember how we crashed and burned.

here's your jersey. I never wanted it anyway. I put it on by accident when I left your house that night. the digital clock our greatest enemy. I loved it then because it smelled like you and you won your game that night. but the blue bled into my favorite white dress and if that's not us in a nutshell, I don't know what is.

you are a stain in my past but somehow you lace the future with heartbreak because the day I broke your heart is a blood stain on my calendar every year. January 22. January 22. January 22.

infinities are for fools. all that matters is what you feel in this instant because tomorrows shift what is in your heart like tremors of an earthquake and I don't trust this planet.

-*(or you)*

the silhouette
of you
standing at the window
is mocking me
will you stay?
probably not
yet my heart is beating out of my chest
at just the sight of
your shoulders
are they cold?
because they sure feel like it
from here
I deserve better
so much better
I deserve magic
but all I got
was a cheap magician

"all I see is red
but everything in that love affair was artificial
so maybe it's red 40"

sea salt and light mist rest upon my face and I can feel her behind me. she touches the back of my arm lightly and everything is gray. the sky. the sea. my heart. I can't feel anything but at the same time I can feel absolutely everything. I can feel my heart jumping and beating and heavy in my chest and I can feel her breath behind me. I turn around and I can't look at her. so I look at her white sundress and then I close my eyes because even that's too much. and behind closed eyelids I can still see when everything was the same. but the word goodbye feels heavy in my mouth and I'm not ready for her to leave.

if it's going to rain
let it pour

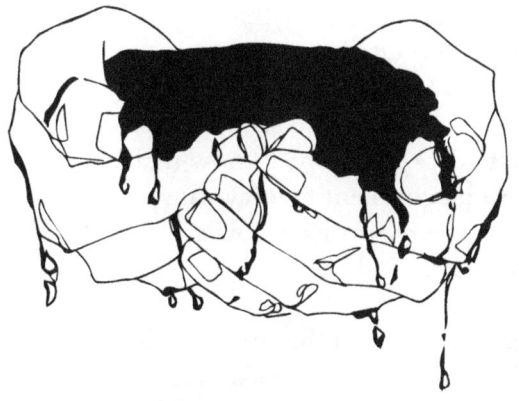

the farther I am distanced, the more that I can breathe
and 30,000 feet above seems like the perfect place to seethe
I'm far above the grass my palms pressed into at the age of nine
I am fairly certain that this will show them my spine
if they even notice I'm gone

flight attendants' questions float past my ears
my doubts are slowly transforming into fears
sweaty cushions and scratchy blankets are all that prevail
what if they don't follow my trail?
passengers are no family

we are just strangers whose lines have crossed
and in the midst of this sky, I know that I am lost
like an object; equivalent to a favorite pen or cell phone
now I must reap what I have sown
a jet is no place to call home

sunbeams filter through the small window
illuminating eyes and making skin glow
I wish I could grab hold of them and let myself down
I'm inclined to turn right back around
these cushions are no cradle

as we touch down, I'm the loneliest I've ever been
in a slow-moving crowd, I feel my sins painted all over my skin
my fingers wrap around the handle of my bag, that's when I see
they are here and I let my tears free
home isn't the airport, it is the arms cradling me

-*runaway*

have you ever been to space?

I've sat on rooftops breathing in smoke of burning stars and so close to planets that I could trace them and they could graze me. I've gazed at galaxies with electricity zipping through my body and snapping and zapping at my fingertips. I've come so close to black holes that I'm surprised I'm still breathing. my eyes have drifted in and out of focus because of my lack of space suit and therefore my lack of oxygen. so yes, I've been to space. but now I've returned.

shattered
scattered
mind
breathing softly
leafing through pages
leaving again
lying (in so many ways)
with my eyes wide open

broken whispers
through closed doors
rattling as I breathe
teardrops don't faze me
anymore

your eyes were once
settling blue marble
but now they're ripped open
galaxies
and I'm sinking
into them

I walked into her bathroom that night, the night of her funeral, the night every one of my family members gathered in a circle on the floor of her living room, talking about anything but her. I walked into her bathroom, and the first thing I noticed was a half-used bottle of mouthwash sitting upon the countertop. my breath slowed as I stared at it, afraid to even reach out and touch it. that tiny plastic bottle made my insides cave in. in that instant, nothing mattered, nothing at all, except for the fact that she would never be able to finish that bottle of mouthwash. the breath that usually swished in and out of my lungs with ease had been stolen from me. I sat down on the lid of the toilet seat and held my head in my hands. a single reminiscence pierced the forefront of my mind, urgently: my father, who I had never seen shed a single tear, stopping short on the night of my last soccer game and bending his head, putting one hand on his stomach while the other clutched mine, and crying softly. who put his forehead on the steering wheel in the car and sobbed, who kept saying, "you only get one mom . . . she was mine." and aching memories flooded my mind: how I didn't cry then, how I didn't cry at her funeral while everyone else around me was weeping into their programs. but I glanced at the bottle of mouthwash, the green translucent liquid that it held, and tears poured down my cheeks. I didn't feel her anywhere, not in that car, not in that church, not even in my father's sobs. the only place I felt her was in that bottle.

-does she know that?

101

the sand in the hourglass
is leaking
from the top
to the bottom
my darling, our time is running out

once upon a time
you kissed me
and stars poured from
your mouth
to mine
and my body turned
to liquid gold
I was precious, priceless

once upon a time
I had the key to your heart
but I seem to have misplaced it

once upon a time
you kept me safe and secure,
far from peril
what happened?
when did you
become the person I am frightened of,
the person who thrusts me in the face
of danger?

once upon a time
in the city that never sleeps
strands of hair blow around my face
and I am numb

-a fairytale

but maybe she was right, and there was a reason
my mother always warned me about flames

-*"come closer"*

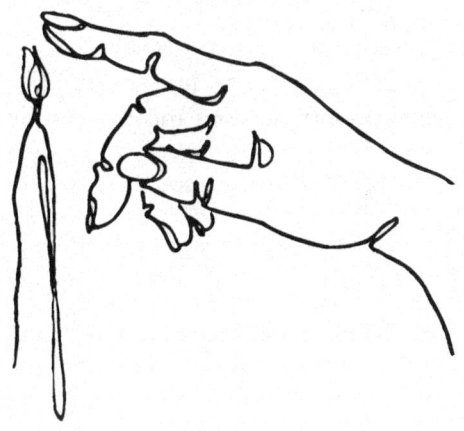

I think every time you love someone it's a little bit different. that boy down the street was puppy love. he represented innocence and everything pure you once were. that boy with the sun tattoo you loved with reckless abandon, all crazy, heat and passion. and the boy with the blue eyes and the half-smile who didn't understand you, yet you still let him make you feel wanted. you weren't addicted to him, but to the way he made you feel. and finally, the boy with the hair like sand and the eyes that remind you of coffee. you love him now, with a certain slowness and sweetness. like stretchy summer nights or chocolate melting in your mouth. you lick your lips after you kiss him.

it's like he was right there. and in a way, he was always right there. distanced by these inches of space that might as well have been miles. he was right there, his arm so close I could feel the warmth radiating off of it. I could see his eyes reflecting the light of the people living within the screen. if these chairs were our homes, we would be neighbors. and I would spend my entire life catching glimpses of him, wondering what it would be like to live in the same place. but things change and eventually we'll move away from these cushioned homes and he will be the reason I don't put out a welcome mat anymore. eventually.

-but it's okay; pretend this night will last forever

as the rain picks up speed, my thoughts do too
and I feel the weight of the clouds on my creaking roof; my
heart feels just as heavy
the sky is sorry and I hope that you know that I am too

-the heavens and I are very similar tonight

the sun drips over the trees
and the shadows elongate
stretching my lies
even further
the sun quickly kisses me goodbye
before blinking
and sinking
below the water
drowning
and now I have
about as much strength
as a paper airplane
I've found everything is louder
in the dark
including silence

-a fractured promise

when you left me, I cried until the white sheets on my bed turned grey, soaked with tears. music with lyrics that could make a poet cry filled my ears. and I was weak. but as the days passed I realized that I will do greater things than having my name attached to yours. and I buried reminders of you in my backyard along with the sheets on my bed because no silly boy should ever be able to run me dry.

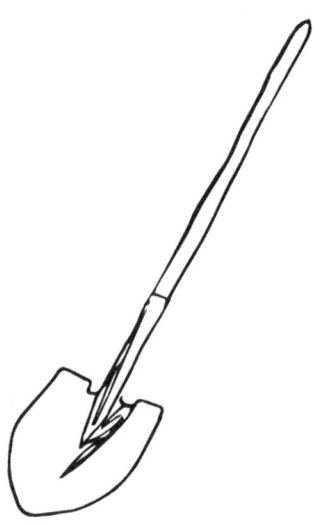

beautiful excuses
and flash tattoos.
fingers uncurling
to the sky.
the pounding bass
like a heartbeat
replacing mine.
smalls of backs sticky
with sweat.
and messy hair
swinging to the beat.
so this is what it feels like
to be alive.

AWAKENING

flowers bloom inside of me like they were always meant to,
nourished by the light of my soul. at first, you cannot see them.
but I am content with that. because I can see them. and as I
continue down the path that my intuition has led me on, they
begin to sprout out of my eyes, they blossom in my mouth.
they sing songs and they emit a sweet smell that is deeply
enchanting. fall away do the things that do not serve me any
longer. but I am grateful for them all the same, because they've
taught me countless lessons. but they cannot exist in this
moment, when I am a garden.

under a tunnel of trees, my heart is humming. my heart strings have just been strummed like a guitar and I can feel the reverberations down to the tips of my toes. I am alone, but I am the farthest thing from lonely. my hair whips around my face and sticks to my lips and it tastes like honey and smells of strawberries. the sun caresses the nape of my neck and I almost fall apart from feeling so whole. but still, amongst the warmth and peace of this golden light, something tugs at the back of my mind. it wraps itself around the tranquility of the moment. how can this same sweet, soft sunlight burn? how can something that kisses me so tenderly sting so severe? yet something tells me that this time is different. this love is different. I turn around so my face catches the beams of light and I am certain: sunlight may scorch but this love that I aim inward will only glow.

you were sculpted with hands that never make mistakes.
you were painted delicately
with graceful strokes, with fluid fingers.
don't let the world smudge you,
don't let it crack your divinity.
once you realize your delicacy,
you are invincible.

I wonder if my soul knew something
that I didn't
when I first laid eyes on you

my love, do you remember, when we were young, how we stumbled along, kissing sloppily. messy, but we held hands always. before we knew it, we had tripped, head over heels, down the rabbit hole. coming out the other side where there was no gravity. we floated among the lights that wander, our lungs saturated with stardust. when I breathed you in, I heard drums: my heart, always musically inclined. I closed my eyes. and all I felt was your voice. it cast rainbows inside my head, your words a kaleidoscope of color. and when I opened them, I was swimming in the shimmering liquid you call your eyes. we are lucky. we are not tethered. gravity does not hold us captive. I am lucky. I can close my eyes and know, that behind closed eyelids, the light I see is you.

-we are a cosmic love

people are not scales
your worth is not measured
by people's misguided
perceptions of you

but the thing is, you are the same as you always were:
ever changing.
you let other people's notions fill your consciousness:
who are you?
what are you like?
as if that makes up the sum of your soul.
why do you assign traits to yourself?
so you are easy to understand?
I prefer to be an enigma.
let people be confused, let them wonder.
because you are so complex,
no one will ever understand the stars you have swirling
inside of you.
the universe you are.
you are so much more than this human form you have taken.
you are not your degree, or the job you choose to take.
you are not simply nice or intelligent or funny.
you are your soul,
which expands far beyond the confines of your mind.

who will I be
if I continue down a path
that is not my own?

-validation

I see a blank piece of paper and I see script written on it, written through it. the words transcend laws of time and matter. I see them and feel them before they exist. they feel me, seep into my consciousness. to write is to become the words themselves. and to feel is to feel every letter. feel their texture, feel their weight. feel how they'll mold to the world around them. and if they don't, then it's the perfect fit.

-to be an artist

what started as a whisper
has now engulfed me in its presence

-intuition

in the faint, flickering candlelight, I dip a paintbrush into a lilac hue, feeling the resonance of a song wrap around me. deep, full notes that I have never encountered before this moment fill me to the brim. and in the pale starlight, I dance. my limbs streaked with paint, a canvas of their own. I dive deeper into a cosmic wonderland, creating an ocean of color from nothingness. and just when time begins to fade away, I blow out the flames, watching the soft indigo smoke draw closer to the sky. returning.

we met by accident but I loved you on purpose.
I think of how, in the blue months, I wasn't even scared. I don't
know how, but with you . . . with you I was fearless. boundless.
limitless. and came the months when the sky stays pink late into
the evening; my hope was faltering. the air was warm and sweet
and I couldn't imagine how something so beautiful could be so
delicate. I tasted salt on my lips when I kissed you for the last
time in that tall grass. it hurt. I don't know how else to put it
that's not honest. it was utterly painful. it (you) left me feeling
untethered. but after you drove away (and after you hit your
steering wheel and cursed loudly into the evening air), I laid
down carefully in that tall grass, looking up into the sky. I felt
as if I could be plucked off the earth's surface at any second,
but gravity pressed me down with its unwavering touch. and
the stars started to peek out from behind their indigo curtain,
one by one; it looked so hauntingly perfect. and I couldn't
understand how the world could look so perfect, so right, when
everything inside me felt so fucking wrong. I stayed in that field
all night, my eyes blurring everything once in a while, but never
sleeping. and as 1:00 descended into 2:00 and the sky deepened
into an inky black, I placed my palms on the ground and closed
my eyes. and for the first time that night, everything in my
mind grew still. and oh, I felt everything. there was such an
enormous release. I began to understand that this life is so
much bigger than this, than me, than you. I smelt the sweet air
and felt it bloom in my lungs. why did the air have to lack its
beauty, its sweetness, just because you were gone? why did I?
why did I have to give up feeling limitless, boundless, fearless,
just because I didn't have your validation any longer?
*we met by accident, but I loved you because your leaving taught
me my own magic.*

I belong
everywhere

my cracks
expose the flowers blooming
beneath my skin

-I've had to break
to realize my beauty

"do you believe in magic?"
"I believe in you, don't I?"

-from me to you . . . from you to me

I am learning to live
softly:
slow-moving beauty
and gentle promises
of love
(silent and everlasting)
I am learning to speak
with a tongue made of
rose petals:
sweet fragrance
and light
leaking from my lips
I am learning to love
differently:
with a heart so whole
it fills my entire chest
with a heart so whole
even before another
claims it
I am learning to understand
myself:
surrendering the words in my mind
that aren't even mine

-I am still understanding how to be

in my soul,
I met God

you ignite fire
in my bones
that have been engulfed
in ice
for so long

time isn't real
but how we perceive it is

-years melt into seconds whenever I'm with you

I am under the covers
under a sheet that reaches past the crown of my head
listening to "I just called to say I love you"
and all around me there is light
and there are shadows
I can bend them
I can shape them
with just the tip of my index finger
and I find beauty in this moment
the simplicity
the contentment
the utter honesty
in how a weight lies between my breasts
deep in my chest
where the base of my heart resides
it is heavy inside of me
the most intimate part
but being surrounded by the contrast of light and dark
seems to have a certain balance to it
and as I move my hands around the sheet that hovers
just above my pupils
I feel the weight in my chest shift to something different
something less solid
something softer

-feeling and healing ("it's okay, I'm here")

breathe.
in - remember your past
and acknowledge the things you have done.
out - let those things go.
your past has never and will never define you.
the here and now.
that is what defines you.
whatever ties you together is not tethered to the past. each
moment is a blank slate and you can shape and sculpt your life
into whatever you want it to be.
inhale worries, but exhale positivity.

-just breathe.

we build heroes in our heads.
one false move,
one little misstep,
and they become a villain.
when they were never even bad
(or particularly good, for that matter) to begin with.
it's much simpler to detach from all expectations.
from all assumptions.
that way,
when someone does something that is pleasing to us,
a little light sheds on them,
and they are brighter in our minds.

thank you for today and thank you for tomorrow
and every day after that
I don't know what they hold in their slippery hands
but I know that you have a plan
and I have a purpose

-prayer

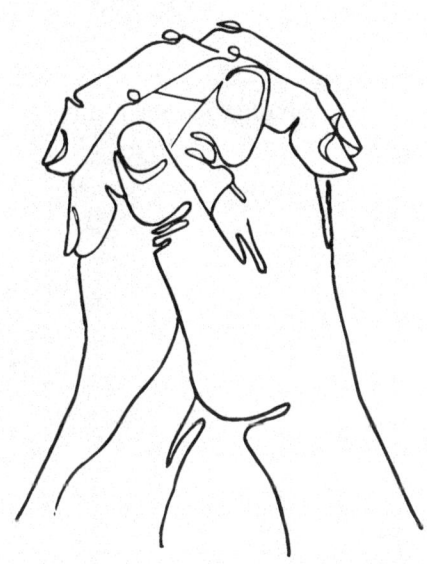

in the jungle, I awoke. droplets of morning dew that had clung to my eyelashes suddenly fell into my eyes, spreading across my irises and making my vision crystal clear. my body uncurled from its dormant position and I stood to my feet. bare. untouched. I felt the earth's lush grass between my toes and beneath the soles of my feet. I took one step, then two. and before I knew it, I was walking, stroking flowers and sucking droplets of honey off the tips of my fingers whenever they ran across it. I trusted everything. it was my most natural state. I felt something bloom in my chest, something like faith. have you ever heard the song in the way the trees rustle and brush together, in the way the wind howls, in the way the sun rises and sets? you haven't been listening close enough. I taste the sweetness in everything. there is honey dripping off the sun. watch me lick it off.

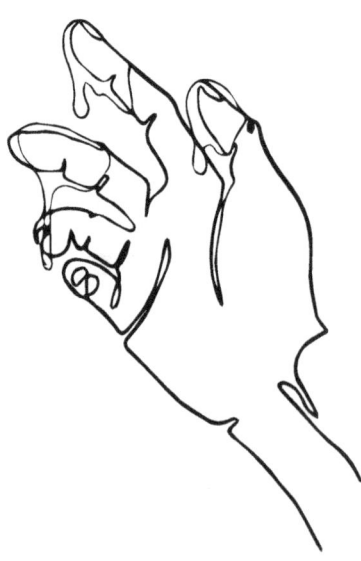

we live beneath a sky
whose blood makes veins
electric
we live on floating chunks of land
that are slowly ripping themselves
apart
we live in between great and vast
nothings

we live within chaos
yet
serenity lives within us

-in a world constantly moving, find stillness Within

it was well past midnight. and I stepped into a taxi with light in my wide eyes and in my full heart. but something shifted in that cab past 12 o'clock. I felt it. the window was rolled down and the summer air had found its way into the backseat. it tangled itself in my hair and made my eyes watery and rimmed them with red. I heard the soft classical notes that floated lightly out the window and into the city. I heard them get lost amongst the sirens and honks. amongst noise that dripped with disconnection. suddenly, my eyes had opened. I felt an overwhelming sensation of pain roll through my body. but it wasn't my pain, it was the pain of the city. the pain of the sky that the buildings so mercilessly scraped, the roads that the tires tirelessly rolled over. the pain of the people tucked away inside a city that is hopelessly sleep deprived. it was the pain of this world. I let my eyes shift to the rearview mirror. I wondered if the driver felt this. or if he had forced himself to desensitize himself to it. because it stung. it burned my skin like a match. like a flame eating through flesh: destroying the surface to truly see beneath. the lights all around me had dimmed. but I felt that I knew something now that other people refused to acknowledge. I saw out of the window, the buildings crumbling down. and I caught the ash in my much too small hands. I curled my fingers into fists, willing the embers to disappear. I closed my eyes. *"this isn't my burden."* but something in the pit of my stomach knew that it was. it is all of ours. I longed to be cradled by the soft earth I felt so deep underneath me. I opened my eyes and unfurled my fingers, letting the ash drift away with the air that rushed past me. I pressed my empty fingers against the hot wind and I felt myself changing against that summer night. my heart was still full, there was still light in my eyes. but it wasn't a lightbulb any longer. it's fire.

home is everywhere
every place my mind can imagine
every place the soles of my feet
touch
because home isn't geography
it isn't a point on a map
home isn't skin and bones
with a heart beat in between
home is deep inside me
where my soul moves
freely

-origins

do you appreciate the way he strokes you when you are alone
like a hand to a fist
he changes that quick
do you love the way he kisses your shoulders
black and blue
who would do that to you
are you fond of the way he holds you close
one hand wrapped around your heart
and the other around your throat
do you like the way he sings you to sleep
tears rolling down your cheeks
his whispers cut deep
but my love,
no matter his efforts to try to convince you
you are yours to keep

I reach inside myself
to find where I am most tender
where I have been told
I am the most broken
and I know
I never have been

audrey emmett

if you took yourself where your bare feet led you, I'd like to
think you would end up somewhere where your soles touched
the earth. where your soul bled into the universe, so, after a
while, you couldn't tell the difference between the two. if you
tilted your head back, you would see fistfuls of stars sprinkled
across the night sky. if you lost yourself in the darkening
heavens, after a while, you'd forget how it feels to see color.
your ego would shrink down and fall away and you'd forget
how it feels to feel superior. hell, you'd forget how it feels to
feel significant. maybe, if everyone took the time to look up
and feel humble, we'd find the answer to most of our problems.

she stands in the middle of an open field, arms open wide and eyes slammed shut. grass brushing her ankles and her dress blowing around her legs. she can hardly remember what it's like to be in a place as busy as her head. clouds rush over her and as the inky black of night pours into day, her arms are still wide open. people have passed by on hikes and bikes, appreciating this day, and they stare, unsure of what she's waiting for. she's not waiting, some argue, she's just appreciating, same as us. they would be correct. she is thanking. thanking for the stars. and for made-up constellations. thanking for small flirty smiles and giant guffaws. and for toddlers that wrap their entire hand around your pointer finger, old bookstores, and giant mugs of tea. she is thanking for baseball and really good cries, for daisies and big cities and finding poetry in people's eyes. for shy hellos and passionate goodbyes. and good artists and bad ones. for concert t-shirts and recipe books that smell like your mother's perfume. she is thankful for the ocean and the land floating in it that we've made our home on. when her arms finally lower and her eyes open slowly, she finds she is not alone. she is surrounded by the hikers and the bikers and the businessmen and women and the artists and the poets and their arms are wide open and they are thankful as well.

-*happy earth day*

don't fall from your place
in the trees
it's a long fall from up there
where the sun brushes your hair
and lights you up
from the inside
where you can see her
rise and set
where the leaves quiver
and tickle your skin
and the moonlight
washes you
where there's no streetlight
to cling to

-*mother nature*

she stopped and stood there, amazed.
in awe of the beauty in front of her
and all around her and inside of her.
that's when it happened.
she began to see the energy she was emitting and the energy of
all the plants and animals, the sentient beings of this planet,
around her. she took in a breath and let one out and saw her
effect on the universe. she realized she *was* the universe. she
was flowing energy, changing every second. she felt magic
coursing through her veins and flooding her heart. she felt love,
deep immense love, pouring into the top of her head in the
form of stardust. the celestial glitter filled her throat and lungs
yet she had never taken a deeper breath than in this moment.
she felt peace. yet vibrancy at the same time. vitality lived in
her. her body was teeming with the most raw, pure, tender life.
her heart had healed itself. she had healed herself. as well as the
world above and below her. and so she whispered *thank you*
and saw the energy of that phrase travel inward and outward,
into the universe.

I am floating, on my back, in a cave. I have been here a very long time. in fact, I cannot remember a time when I was not here. I can feel the water surrounding me, but I hardly notice it. I am so focused on trying to get out of this cavern. but I am not moving. I am stagnant. it frightens me. I do not notice anything in this cave, I only notice that I cannot be somewhere else. but, all of the sudden, I feel the beginning of a wave rolling under me. it is coming towards me, a power I cannot stop or control. all at once, it forces me underwater and I cannot breathe. I am lost under a rushing sea. but I realize something. now. I am moving. though it is not me that is doing the work. it is the swirl of the sea. so I surrender. and. as soon as I stop resisting, the flow brings me to the surface again. I am still in the cave. but this time, I look around. I see her. she is beautiful. the waves have washed the walls of this chamber. I see them. they are diamonds, and they are gem stones of every color in the spectrum. they are colors that do not exist. I feel my heart opening and gratitude spilling from it, into the water I am immersed in. I see around my arms and legs the sea is soft and glowing. she is cradling me. she is telling me I am okay. she knows this had to happen. I feel my tears mixing with the salty ocean. they are one and the same: cleansing. then I see something unexpected: the waves have eroded part of the cavern. there is an opening. there is light. and I realize that I can move. I can swim towards it. but I don't. I let her take me there. I trust her. she knows I'm ready.

there is no escaping the sunlight
it lingers just beneath the darkness
giving the obscurity
illumination
giving the trembling shadows
their magnificence
I see your light
I see your darkness
I kiss them both
with the same lips
with the same tenderness
my love
before you understood
the majesty
of your broken pieces
(sewn together by thin threads of light)
you set fire to the shadows
thinking you could burn
the darkness
so only light would remain
but your spirit fell to ashes
with gold flecks lost in between
but I saw you
my eyelashes dripping with soft tears
you learned to rise
to soar
from nothing.
to everything.

THE LOVE
THE SOUL
THE REFUGE
THE REASON

YOU

you. thank you. I love you. if you have reached the end of these pages, know that you have cradled me in your hands. you have made a home for me in your heart. you have seen me. for who I truly was and am and pray to be. you have seen my memories and my dreams and my consciousness. all interwoven together. you have seen everything. at once. and for that, you have set me free.

I am so touched by you. we are connected now by something that transcends time and distance. I am sure of it. yet, still, I ache to hold you, to embrace you, to promise what you mean to me. I am so grateful for you in ways I cannot form words to explain. my spirit expands to engulf you in nothing but love and gratitude.

vulnerability feels like everything inside of me has cracked wide open. all my soft light is spilling out. but my darkness is also exposed. it is scary in the best way possible. for everyone has darkness, it's what makes us human. for everyone has light, it's what makes us ethereal. we don't have to choose one or the other. we are everything. it is what connects us, it is what makes us one.

I am home. when I write, when I create, I am home. I melt into the moment, making my refuge in the endless possibilities of this vast, beautiful language. and beyond that, I am awake. I know that when I write, though the words are flowing from my body, it is not me writing. it is flowing through me from something higher than me. it is my soul. my highest self. you are holding my dream, my heart, my truth in your hands right now. thankful doesn't begin to scratch the surface of what I am. I am eternally grateful for your love, for your grace. I love you so much. thank you.

you and I, we are here. exactly where we need to be.
we are awake.
we are everything at once.

acknowledgements

thank you. for you have helped me remember my dream. for
you have helped me to awaken.
for you are everything at once, to me.

thank you, to my beautiful mother. who heard me.
when I was bouncing off the walls with excitement about these
words. when I was banging my head against them with
frustration about these words. who was endlessly patient and
helpful even though I wouldn't let her read it until the very end.
who encouraged me to breathe life into this dream. I love you.
thank you.

thank you, to my illustrators. flow and liann. thank you
for creating images that perfectly reflected what I pictured in
my mind. for helping me tell these stories in a whole new way.
you are ever so lovely. I am in awe of your talent and the light
that shines through your art.

thank you, to my entire family. to my father, who
looked at me with such love and support when I told him I was
writing a book. to my cousins and aunts and uncles and
grandparents, who grabbed hold of my hands and told me they
would buy a million copies. I love you. so much.

thank you, to the woman who is like my sister. who has
been (and will be) supporting me forever. I love you.

thank you, to you. to the one who traces these words
with eyes filled with light and a heart to match. you have
tendrils of grace spiraling from your soul. I see you. I love you.
thank you.

all the love and light in the universe,
audrey emmett

about the author

audrey emmett was born at 5:59 am on a monday. ever since she was a little girl, when her nose wasn't buried deep in a book, she has been etching her dreams onto paper. she is, above all else, a writer and an artist. *everything at once* is her first book. audrey pulls inspiration from heart ache, her bouts with depression and anxiety, the grief of loss, and the liberation of finding oneself. when she isn't consuming excessive amounts of tea and pouring her heart out onto paper, she enjoys traveling, escaping into an enchanting novel, meditating, and tapping into her creative flow, whatever that might be. although writing is her first great love, photography, painting, along with other forms of self-expression entice her as well. audrey is currently a student, living in the beautiful bay area of california, but in a few years . . . who knows? she finds beauty in the uncertainty of this life.
she is ever changing. ever growing. always dreaming.

connect with her on instagram/twitter: @audrey_emmett

you can visit her website: audreyemmett.com

CPSIA information can be obtained
at www.ICGtesting.com
Printed in the USA
LVHW031937160622
721466LV00002B/395